SOARING WITH
THE EAGLES

Kenneth Hagin Jr.

Unless otherwise indicated, all Scripture quotations in this volume are from the *King James Version* of the Bible.

Second Printing 2006

ISBN 0-89276-734-0

In the U.S. write:	In Canada write:
Kenneth Hagin Ministries	Kenneth Hagin Ministries
P.O. Box 50126	P.O. Box 335, Station D
Tulsa, OK 74150-0126	Etobicoke (Toronto), Ontario
1-888-28-FAITH	Canada, M9A 4X3
www.rhema.org	www.rhemacanada.org

Contents

Chapter 1
Learning a Lesson From the Eagle

The eagle. What an incredible creature in flight! Effortlessly, he glides through the open skies, commanding the respect of all who look on. Then with a flap of his great wings, he leaves the world far behind as he soars upward to breathtaking heights.

What makes this bird so regal, so majestic? What is it about him that is so impressive? And why would God compare Himself and us to the eagle in Scripture?

There is obviously something significant about the eagle. And I believe we can gain some insight about God and ourselves by taking a closer look at this remarkable bird that God created!

God Has Made Himself Plain Through Creation

The truth is, we can learn lessons not only from the eagle, but from all of God's Creation. In the Book of Romans, Paul tells us that nature itself reveals to us that God exists. Much of what we can know about God is "shown" or "made plain" through the very things He made.

ROMANS 1:19,20
19 Because that which may be known of God is manifest in them; for God hath SHEWED it unto them.
20 For the invisible things of him from the creation of the world are clearly seen, being understood by the things that are made, even his eternal power and Godhead; so that they are without excuse.

ROMANS 1:19,20 (NIV)
19 Since what may be known about God is plain to them, because GOD HAS MADE IT PLAIN to them.
20 For since the creation of the world God's invisible qualities — his eternal power and divine nature — have been clearly seen, being understood from what has been made, so that men are without excuse.

So you see, man has no excuse for not believing in God. Why? Because according to these verses of Scripture, nature clearly shows us that there is a Higher Power, which we know to be God.

Man Stands Alone in God's Creation

The Bible says that God is the Creator and that the heavens and the earth and every living thing in it were made by Him (Isa. 40:28; Gen. 1:1-31).

It's hard to imagine how anyone can look at the magnificence of this universe and come anywhere close to believing the theory that this world began as a speck which developed while floating through time.

Then others believe that the entire universe came into being through some cataclysmic explosion in outer space! Those who hold to this theory say that after the big explosion, every star, galaxy, and celestial body fell perfectly into place and just happened to end up the exact number of miles apart they needed to be! And then "by chance" the spin or rotation of these celestial bodies created just the right amount of gravitational pull necessary for each planet to keep its position in the galaxy and not float off somewhere in space! Isn't that fantastic!

There are also some pretty amazing theories about how man came into being. For example, some say that every animal in existence (and they include man) evolved from a one-celled amoeba. But when I look at man and I see how divinely and fitly he's made, it's amazing to me that anyone could think man evolved from a microscopic organism.

Think about it. If man really did evolve over millions of years from an amoeba or from other species of animals, then with all the years that have passed, at least some kind of evidence of evolution between species would have been discovered by now — but it hasn't!

No, man stands alone. The Bible says that man was created by God, in God's own image and in His likeness (Gen. 1:26). And God reveals Himself to man through the wonders of His Creation.

Nature's Object Lessons

The Bible often uses nature to teach practical lessons and to illustrate certain truths. For example, according to Proverbs 6:6-8, you can study the ant and learn something about self-motivation, hard work, and planning. And in the Book of Matthew, Jesus talks about the lilies of the field and the birds of the air to describe how God takes care of and provides for His children (Matt. 6:25-30; 10:29-31).

Then there are other scriptures, like the ones we'll concentrate on in this book, that use the eagle as an illustration. Notice in particular this passage in Deuteronomy.

> DEUTERONOMY 32:11,12
> 11 AS AN EAGLE stirreth up her nest, fluttereth over her young, spreadeth abroad her wings, taketh them, beareth them on her wings:
> 12 So the Lord alone did lead him [Israel], and there was no strange god with him.

I think it's interesting to note that out of all the birds that could have been mentioned, this scripture said, "As an EAGLE. . . ."

You see, the eagle has certain characteristics that set it apart from all other birds in Creation. And I believe we can learn some things by studying this interesting creature. So are you ready to learn a lesson from the eagle?

Chapter 2
The Majestic Eagle

The eagle has been used as a symbol of majesty for centuries. The early Romans used its emblem on their shields of battle because it was the recognized symbol of the Roman Empire. It was also used by the ancient Greeks and Egyptians. And the national symbol for the United States of America is the American bald eagle, with a sprig of olive branches clutched in its right talon and a band of arrows in its left.

Noted for Its Strength

Not only does the eagle symbolically stand for majesty, but it also stands for strength, because an eagle is extremely strong. For example, an eagle can swoop down from the sky, pick up an animal off the ground that weighs as much as or more than it does, and fly off with that animal in its talons.

Now when most people first think of a bird, they may think of a duck or some other small bird that doesn't weigh more than a few pounds. But eagles are large fowl that can weigh as much as fifteen pounds, with wing spans that can extend more than seven feet! Those huge wings give eagles a great deal of strength, especially when it comes to their unique ability in flight.

No other bird can soar as high as the eagle does; no other bird even comes close to ascending to great heights like the eagle. An eagle will sometimes fly to heights of more than 10,000 feet!

In fact, when an eagle builds its nest, it often flies way up into the highest part of a mountain cliff.

The Eagle Nest

An eagle nest is absolutely like no other bird's nest you may have ever seen. The male and female eagles use extremely large sticks and branches to build their nest.

The eagles take these large branches high up on the mountain and begin to arrange them inside the cleft of a rock. After that, they begin to add smaller branches. Next they line the nest with leaves. Then as the final step, the eagles may take downy feathers that have fallen off their own bodies to cover the inside of the nest.

Once it's finished, an eagle nest is very soft inside.

Now I want you to notice *where* the eagles build their nest. They take all the materials that they gather up on the mountain, and they build their nest on the *rocks*.

There is a lesson here we need to consider. For example, look at what Jesus said in Matthew 7 about building upon a rock.

MATTHEW 7:24
24 Therefore whosoever heareth these sayings of mine, and doeth them, I will liken him unto a wise man, which BUILT HIS HOUSE UPON A ROCK.

Notice Jesus said that a wise man builds his house upon a rock. Why? Because a rock is one of the strongest foundations anyone can build upon — especially when it's solid rock!

So we can learn a lesson from the eagle when it comes to building a strong framework or "spiritual house" for our lives. You see, just as the eagle builds its nest on a solid foundation, it's important that we build our spiritual lives upon one too!

The foundation is the most important part of any construction because it's the base. So the foundation needs to be strong; it needs to be sturdy and sure. And if you're going to fulfill what God has planned for your life, you have to build on the only sure foundation — Jesus Christ, the Rock (1 Cor. 10:4). Unless you do, nothing that you do for the Lord will be able to stand.

Able To Withstand the Storm

Now I want you to realize that the eagles are not just building some little, bitty ole nest. This is a large construction, weighing sometimes as much as two tons and well able to weather the elements.

If you know anything about mountains, you know that the strongest gusts of wind usually form near the peaks because of the high altitudes. But an eagle nest can withstand those forceful winds because it's built inside the cleft of a rock. Those eagles build their nests to stay!

That's what *we* need to do. We need to build a place of permanence in the cleft of the rock — the Rock,

Christ Jesus — so that when the winds and the storms of life come, our spiritual dwelling will remain established firmly on that solid foundation.

A House Built on the Word Will Stand!

In the very midst of the storm, the male and female eagles snuggle down in their nest, knowing that they're secure — because they've built their nest properly to begin with. In the same way, when you get hold of God's Word and you build your life correctly on the foundation of His Word, you, too, can be secure.

The devil can howl all he wants. The unfavorable circumstances and the storms of life can come. But you'll snuggle down firmly in your spiritual house, knowing that it will stand and that nothing that comes against it can destroy it. But, you see, that kind of security only comes from knowing what God's Word says and then building your life on the solid foundation of the Word!

There is a classic children's story called "The Three Little Pigs" that reminds me of the illustration Jesus used of a man who built his house on the rock and a man who built his house on the sand (Matt. 7:24-27; Luke 6:47-49).

As the story goes, there once were three little pigs who each built a house. The first little pig built a house out of straw, and the second little pig built a house made of wood. But the third little pig built his house with brick.

Well, you can't build a brick house overnight — it takes time! But the first two pigs didn't want to spend a lot of time on their houses. They wanted to do other things, so they just threw something together. However, the third Brother Pig took time to build a strong, solid house (and if it hadn't been for his compassion, he would have been the only little pig that survived!).

This smart little pig built his house in such a way that it would stand the test. And no sooner had he finished it then the big bad wolf — let's say, the devil — came and yelled, "I'm going to blow your house in!"

Well, the little pig said, "You can huff and you can puff all you want to, Mr. Wolf. I've built a strong house, and you can't blow my house down!" You see, that little pig was secure!

Now when the enemy comes against some people, they begin to tremble and shake because they're really not secure. They don't know if their house will stand the test.

But if you're secure in knowing that you've built a strong spiritual house upon what the Word of God says, you can stand against the enemy and say with confidence, "Do what you will, Mr. Devil, but I shall stand because I've built my house upon God's Word!"

Take the Time To Build Right

That's the type of confidence that the eagle displays. Whether in flight or safely snuggled in his nest, the majestic eagle will stare a storm in the face and defy it.

If he's not airborne, he'll hunker down in his nest as if to say, "Blow all you want to, wind. Blizzard, come on! I'll remain firm because I took the time to build my nest properly."

But the problem with some Christians is that they haven't taken the time to build their lives properly on the Word. Then when the enemy hits them, they have to go back and start construction all over again.

Do you know that it's harder to *rebuild* something than it is to build it right the first time? Just talk to anyone who knows anything about construction. They'll tell you that it's cheaper, easier, and a whole lot more practical to construct a building right the first time, than it is to go back and have to redo it later.

Well, if that's true in building a natural house or dwelling, how much more is it going to be true when you build your spiritual house — your framework for a life of faith in God? I tell you, you'd better build your spiritual house right the first time because when the devil comes in, sometimes you don't have time for a reconstruction project. He'll attack and try to destroy your faith before you can even get started. But thank God, you don't have to worry if you've taken the time to build your house on the Word, right from the start!

The Father's Job Is To Provide

When the male and female eagle complete their nest, they're then ready to start their family. (Another interesting characteristic about eagles is that they mate for life — but that's another whole lesson that I won't go into now!)

Sometime in the spring, the mama eagle lays one or two eggs, which hatch after a few weeks. From the time she lays those eggs until after they've hatched, the papa eagle spends his time providing for the needs of his family. Then when the newly hatched chicks begin to feather, the mother eagle helps the father eagle provide food for the developing eaglets.

Now here is something we can see from God's Word as we learn another lesson from the eagle. The Bible instructs the Christian man to provide for his family as the head of his household. It tells him to put his wife and children first and his own personal needs, wants, and desires second (Eph. 5:25-29; 1 Tim. 5:8).

But then on the other hand, when you look at this lesson from the spiritual standpoint, we are in *God's* family now through the New Birth. And God said that *He* will provide for us.

PHILIPPIANS 4:19
19 But my GOD SHALL SUPPLY all your need according to his riches in glory by Christ Jesus.

PSALM 37:25
25 I have been young, and now am old; YET HAVE I NOT SEEN THE RIGHTEOUS FORSAKEN, NOR HIS SEED [God's children] **BEGGING BREAD.**

God is the Heavenly Father of all who are born again; therefore, He is our Provider! Hallelujah!

The Father's Abundance

As soon as the little baby eagles hatch out of their eggs, the papa eagle will bring home to the nest what appear to be gifts. Scientists and wildlife experts haven't figured out why this happens; the male eagle just does this for no apparent reason.

Of course, the father eagle still brings food for the sustenance of his family, but he also starts bringing home little "extras," such as old tin cans and other unusual articles that he happens to find.

You see, sometimes fathers get a little overexuberant when their children are born, and they bring home all kinds of gifts that really aren't necessary. I know I've been guilty of that. And I'm sure some other dads have too — especially *first-time* fathers and grandfathers!

Mama might say, "What is that?"

Dad says, "Oh, just a little something I wanted to bring home for the baby."

"But what can the baby do with it?"

"I don't know. I just thought it would be nice."

Well, it would seem that what *we* do as dads when our children are born is similar to the papa eagle's behavior. And I believe we can compare the eagle's conduct with the way God liberally provides for *His* children!

You see, God cares about more than just providing for our needs; He wants to give us some other pleasures as well. He wants to shower us with blessings and every good gift (Ezek. 34:26; James 1:17).

I've heard people say, "I just can't figure it out. Sometimes it seems as if God just blesses me for no reason at all. I don't understand why He would treat me as if I were so special."

Well, you don't have to understand it. You don't have to try to figure it out. Just know that God loves His children, and He takes great pleasure in providing more for them than just the things they need!

Chapter 3
Time To Fly!

AS AN EAGLE STIRRETH UP HER NEST,
fluttereth over her young, spreadeth abroad her
wings, taketh them, beareth them on her wings:
So the Lord alone did lead him [Israel]. . . .
— Deuteronomy 32:11,12

After the baby eagles hatch out of their eggs, they have it easy for a while. They sit in their soft, downy nest, and everything that they need in life is brought to them. But one day, things change. There comes a day when the mother eagle stirs up the nest!

Stirring Up the Nest

On that day, the mama eagle gets down in the nest and begins to flap and flutter her wings, making those little baby eagles get up and walk around. Then she may start taking away all the soft leaves and downy feathers so the eaglets can't get comfortable — when her young ones try to lie down, the sticks prick them. You see, it's time for the babes to grow up!

You may be at the same place in your spiritual walk. God has provided for you and helped you along.

15

But you've heard enough Word now, and it's time for you to grow up spiritually. It's time for you to start believing God's Word on your own.

Sometimes people reach a place in their walk with the Lord where they wonder why things are not as comfortable as they used to be. Well, it may be that they need to grow up! It may be that God is stirring them just as a mama eagle stirs up her nest and flutters over her young!

That's what the Lord may be doing with you. He's fluttering over you. He's taking away all the downy feathers — all the things in your life that make it easy to stay spiritually complacent. He's trying to help you get up to begin to move out of your comfort zone and learn how to believe Him for yourself (and not just for *yourself*, but also for *others!*).

Free-Falling

Now after a few days of stirring up her baby eaglets and making them walk around in the prickly nest, the mother gets in the nest behind them and flutters her wings until one of the eaglets finally climbs up on the rim of the nest.

But the mother eagle doesn't stop there. With the fluttering of her wings, she deliberately crowds him onto the rim and right off the edge. And there goes the tiny little eagle, free-falling!

You may be thinking, *Brother, that's me! I feel like I've just been pushed over the edge of my comfortable life, and I'm free-falling. So what am I supposed to do now?*

You have to do what you've seen other Christians do — use your "faith wings" and start believing God!

The Heavenly Father Will Not Let You Fall!

That poor little eagle. The only thing he knows to do is what he's seen mama and papa do with those massive wings of theirs every time they came flying down to the nest. So the eaglet starts flapping his little wings — but it's not helping a whole lot. Then just before he hits the ground, the mama or papa eagle swoops right underneath him and gently bears the little eagle on its great wings back to the nest.

I love that. You may be on the ledge, so to speak, looking down on a situation that seems impossible. You may be in midair, trying out your wings of faith for the very first time. You may look as though you're about to hit rock bottom and then it'll all be over. But friend, I want to tell you that the Heavenly Father will not let you fall (Exod. 19:4)!

Learning How To Fly

I want us to look at how Deuteronomy 32:11 reads in the *New International Version*.

DEUTERONOMY 32:11 (NIV)
11 Like an eagle that stirs up its nest and hovers over its young, that spreads its wings to catch them and carries them on its PINIONS.

I looked up that word "pinion" in the dictionary, and it means *a bird's wing*. Actually it's the post-lateral section of a bird's wing. That's where the little bird lands: on the pinion of his parent's wing.

Well, do you know what? The very next day, the eagles go through the same thing all over again. But this time the eaglet is much stronger and he flies a little bit longer before he has to be borne up on his parent's wings.

Then after about three days of this exercise, all of a sudden it happens: The little eagle begins to soar majestically on the thermal and on the wind with outspread wings. He's flying!

I can just picture him as he flies through the air. He's looking around at God's wonderful Creation, thinking, "Oh, man, this is fun!"

The same thing happens when *you* first jump out of the security of your spiritual nest and begin to believe God. It's not too much fun at first. But once you really learn how to fly — how to trust and believe God in every situation of life — you wouldn't have it any other way!

After a while, your faith wings become strengthened because you've been constantly exercising them. Then you have no problem at all when you come up against a chasm of tests or trials — because you're used to relying on God's Word. So you jump right out in the middle of that great gulf, knowing that God's Word is going to hold you up and bear you safely to the other side.

Well, somewhere around the fifth day, the mama eagle doesn't even have to nudge her young one out of the nest anymore. Instead, they get up and fly off together!

Don't Be Afraid
To Try Your Wings!

If you're ever going to soar with the eagles, you have to be willing to trust God and leave the security of the nest. And if you're ever going to receive the things you believe God has spoken to your heart and see them come to pass, you have to be willing to try your spiritual wings. (They're there; you just may not know they are!)

That little eagle's wings were there all the time — he just didn't know what to do with them! But the mother knew exactly when it was time for her young one to spread his own wings and learn to fly.

In the same way, you need to learn to trust God because *He* knows when it's time for *you* to start spreading your own spiritual wings and learn how to live by faith in His Word.

It's all part of growing up spiritually. You can't always remain in the nest of safety. Sooner or later you have to learn how to step out in faith. You have to get out of the nest and learn to fly!

You see, many people are not going to get any more direction from God until they first make a move. I'm not talking about moving out of town or moving to another church. I'm talking about moving on with God and developing their faith.

Sometimes folks come to a place in their Christian lives where it seems like they just don't know where to go or what to do. It's as if they're stymied in their spiritual growth. And I believe one reason is that they haven't moved on with God. They haven't developed their faith.

So you see, you're going to have to make a move. You're going to have to step out of your nest of spiritual dependence and complacency and learn to trust God. Don't be afraid to try your wings of faith. You have the potential to *soar* on those wings, and one day you will — but not unless you make a move and take that first step!

Take Off the Limits!

God will never limit you from receiving all He has for you. The truth is, *you* are the one who limits God in your life!

Let me ask you a question. How big can you dream for God — how much can you believe Him for? Your answer to that question will determine your spiritual altitude or how high you will soar in life with Christ.

The limit is yours, not God's. Study the Word and you'll see that God doesn't put any limits on you.

He says, ". . . *nothing shall be impossible unto you*" (Matt. 17:20). *He* says, ". . . *What things soever ye desire, when ye pray, believe that ye receive them, and ye shall have them*" (Mark 11:24)!

In other words, God says, "You can have *whatever* you can believe for according to My Word." Therefore, that puts any limitations back on you as to how far you can go in God!

The Word of God says it this way in Philippians 4:13: "*I can do ALL things through Christ which strengtheneth me.*" That "I" means *you*, if you'll take God at His Word.

It's up to you how high you will soar in life. So take off the limits and set your sights high in God. Learn a lesson from the eagle: Build your spiritual house on the right foundation — on the Word — and build it strong so it will stand the test. Then don't be afraid to step out in faith and try your spiritual wings. It's something *you* have to do. Your mother, your father, your sister, or your brother can't do it for you. God Himself can't even do it for you.

You have to learn to believe God and take Him at His Word. But if you will, pretty soon you'll find yourself flying over the chasm of impossibilities with nothing underneath your feet but God's Word. And you'll find yourself soaring to greater heights than you ever thought you could attain!

Dare To Believe God!

Jesus said, *"Heaven and earth shall pass away, but my words shall not pass away"* (Matt. 24:35; Mark 13:31; Luke 21:33)!

I am living proof that the Word of God will never fail. In the midst of many seemingly impossible situations, I've had to stand on God's Word and keep on quoting His promises — and I'm still here. I'm still going strong.

I can remember the day many years ago that I sat staring out the window of my office on the RHEMA campus. Bills were piling up, and I felt as if I were carrying the entire weight of having to run a ministry and

Bible school on my shoulders. The devil was screaming in my ears, "You've torn apart what it took your father forty-some-odd years to build!"

But even though the pressure was on, I didn't buckle under because I knew I had built my spiritual house on the foundation of God's Word — and God's Word never fails!

Right there in my office, I made a decision to believe God and stand in faith on His Word. And just to make my point, I put my Bible on the floor and literally stood on it! Then I said, "Mr. Devil, I'll have you know that RHEMA Bible Training Center was not my own idea. It was not my father's idea. It was *God's* idea, and I'm doing what *He* has said. Therefore, God's Word tells me that *He* will supply all my need according to His riches in glory by Christ Jesus [Phil. 4:19]!

"So if God said it, I believe it, and that settles it! I already see it done. I see every bill paid and every need met!" And praise God, to this day, all the bills involved with running the training center have always been met as God has faithfully honored His Word!

Then when we were in the process of building the new RHEMA Bible Church auditorium, people told me that I was crazy to invest as much money as I did in that building. But now they stand back and marvel.

Today we have a beautiful facility, and God blessed us by helping us reduce our mortgage by almost seventy percent in less than five years! I give God the praise for all that's been accomplished. It's all because of Him. But, you see, it was made possible because I dared to step out of my secure nest and try my wings of faith. I dared to take the limits off God and to take Him at His Word when circumstances looked impossible!

Sure, it would have been easier and a lot more comfortable to build a smaller building. But God knew how much space we would need. Already our new sanctuary is full on Sunday mornings, and we're continuing to grow!

So you see, I could have gone with what *man* said, but I chose to go with what *God* said!

I want to encourage you to get hold of what God says and hold on to it. Be tenacious about it. But first you need to make sure you've built your spiritual life on the sure foundation of the Word, because tests and trials *will* come. I've had them come my way, but I've learned to believe God's Word. And the only limits I've had in overcoming those tests are the ones *I've* put on God.

Move Up to Another Level of Faith

God is asking you, "What can you believe Me for?" That's a question you need to realistically ask yourself. In other words, recognize where your level of faith is and determine what you can honestly believe God for right now. Next, start exercising your faith to receive those things that you're believing God for. As you consistently receive the answers to those things, your faith will strengthen and increase, and you can begin to move up to another level of faith.

We should keep moving up to new levels of faith with God's Word until Jesus comes back (then we won't have to believe God anymore for earthly provisions because we'll be with Him!). But in the time that we still have on earth, we can always accomplish more for the Kingdom of God if we'll just step out on the Word and dare to believe God!

Soar on Wings Like Eagles

Sometimes in life it can seem easier to stay in an uncomfortable nest than to step out and start believing God for yourself. You might think your faith wings are too weak to sustain you when it's time to jump out of the nest and fly. But the Bible says God gives power to the faint, and He increases the strength of those who have no might!

> **ISAIAH 40:28-31**
> **28 Hast thou not known? hast thou not heard, that the everlasting God, the Lord, the Creator of the ends of the earth, fainteth not, neither is weary? there is no searching of his understanding.**
> **29 HE GIVETH POWER TO THE FAINT; AND TO THEM THAT HAVE NO MIGHT HE INCREASETH STRENGTH.**
> **30 Even the youths shall faint and be weary, and the young men shall utterly fall:**
> **31 But they that wait upon the Lord shall RENEW THEIR STRENGTH; they shall MOUNT UP WITH WINGS AS EAGLES; they shall run, and not be weary; and they shall walk, and not faint.**

Now the eagle does not have tremendous power in his wings to begin with; his wings have to be *developed*!

Remember that when an eaglet first learns to fly, his mother pushes him out of the nest and off the edge, and he goes tumbling thousands of feet, trying to flop his little wings. Then the mama or papa eagle swoops underneath him, catches him, and bears him back up to the nest.

They go through this exercise time and time again until one day, after falling a little ways, all of a sudden, the little eagle begins to mount up and soar on strengthened wings.

Well, that's what we need to do. We need to keep using our wings of faith, prayer, and praise until we begin to soar on the winds of the Holy Spirit with our Heavenly Father.

So you see, you don't have the power to soar with spiritual wings to begin with — you have to develop them first. How? By strengthening them! By constantly exercising your faith in God's Word and spending time every day with the Lord in prayer and praise.

It's time to fly! It doesn't matter if you're teetering on the edge of your nest of safety, stepping out on God's Word for the very first time, or if you've already discovered your faith wings. God will not let you fall and His Word will never fail you!

Friend, don't be afraid to climb out of that familiar nest and use your spiritual wings. Take off the limits and dare to believe God again and again until living by faith in His Word becomes second nature to you. Then before long, you'll begin to mount up with greater confidence and strength on spiritual wings, soaring higher and higher as you reach new altitudes of faith in God!

Chapter 4
The Eagle in the Storm

I want to share excerpts from an account of a man who personally witnessed the courage of an eagle in a storm. I believe his story effectively illustrates two things we can learn from the eagle.

> A thunderbolt of lightning flashed vividly across the dark sky.... Dark forboding clouds rolled across the bay like some giant, sinister, wave of evil. They swirled low to the ground adding dramatically to the already eerie effect. Again a flash of lightning streaked the sky, striking the earth with such devastating power that it caused the house to tremble under the impact.... Branches whisked aloft, trees groaned while leaves and papers catapulted skyward like miniature flying carpets.[1]

The writer goes on to say that while he observed this storm, he noticed different flocks of birds as they huddled in terror, trying to find a place of security. Then he looked way up in the heavens, and soaring against the face of the storm was a magnificent eagle. This eagle whirled and dived through the flashes of lightning. And when the thunder crashed, the eagle would give a flap of his wings and soar on an updraft, even higher into the sky.

> Momentarily I forgot the ferocity of the squall as I
> stood in awe of this magnificent creature of the sky,
> this winged warrior.... Here at last was a creature
> undaunted, unafraid and unaffected by the sheer
> ferocity of the elements.... Indeed, the bird's air of
> tranquility appeared to mock the storm, to dare the
> elements, as it enjoyed the thrill of riding the tur-
> bulent air currents, sailing above them with grace
> and control.[2]

I don't know if you've ever seen a storm like the one
this story talks about, but I used to see them all the
time as a kid growing up in Texas. If you live in an area
where there are a lot of tornadoes, you've probably
experienced severe thunderstorms like that yourself.

Where I come from, those kinds of storms usually
come rolling in around the spring of the year. Sometimes
the claps of thunder are so powerful that they vibrate
the whole house. If you're outside, you can see the birds
fly for cover almost in terror, trying to escape the storm.
You can barely hear yourself talk because the wind is
howling so loud. And everyone starts running for cover
because they know there's a storm coming!

But I want you to notice two things in particular as
we look at the eagle in this story. First, the eagle was
utterly *fearless* in the face of destruction. And second,
he was able to *soar above* all the confusion, the turmoil,
and the fierceness of the storm.

While every other fowl of the air was scurrying for
cover, the eagle confronted the storm and remained at
peace. He stared the storm in the face as if to dare it to
try and harm him.

An eagle will actually do that. Sometimes even in the most fierce storm, the eagle will fly anyway. He will defy the storm!

Now here is something we can learn. In the storms of life, we can be like the other birds and flee in terror or "flap our wings" with all of our *natural* strength as we look for a way to escape trouble. Or we can be like the eagle, staring the storm in the face as we use our wings of faith, prayer, and praise to lift us above the clouds into the realm of peace and tranquillity.

You see, the devil will try to throw everything he can at you, just as the howling winds toss leaves, paper, and debris in your face in a natural storm. But if you learn to develop your wings of faith, then instead of being blown away by the storm, you'll just ride on its updrafts and soar above the clouds! Instead of running in terror, you'll ascend to the heights of victory!

Facing the Storm Head On

You don't ever have to be afraid of the circumstances of life or the challenging situations you may find yourself in. You can always be at peace, because the Bible says there is no fear in him whose mind is stayed on Christ Jesus (Isa. 26:3).

You see, it's up to *you* how you react to the storms of life that come your way. It's *your* decision whether or not you flee in terror or begin to wring your hands and say, "Oh, my Lord! Why is this happening to me?"

We've all been there at one time or another: We've all cowered in the face of trouble and wrung our hands, wondering, *What am I going to do now?*

But thank God, those days are gone! No longer do we have to flee in terror from the enemy. We can rise to victory! We can rise to our full potential in the spiritual realm where God wants us to dwell.

God is not in favor of His people being taken advantage of by the enemy. Consider how the eagle reacts to the storm. Yes, there is turbulence in the storm. Yes, there is the risk of destruction in the storm. And yes, there is the possibility of total devastation. But because of his strength and ability in flight, the eagle keeps the storm from devastating *him*!

You see, the eagle knows what to do in the midst of a storm. He knows exactly when to turn and when to rise and fall with the currents of the wind. So even though the eagle faces a force that could potentially destroy him, he isn't paralyzed by what the storm can do. Why? Because the eagle has confidence in knowing what *he* can do.

Friend, you and I don't need to be so ignorant as to think that potential danger doesn't exist when we face tribulations. Certainly we need to realize that the enemy is a force that can destroy us if we allow him to. But when we know what God's Word has to say, we can follow the wisdom in His Word to know exactly which way to move and what direction to take. Then we can operate with confidence in the storms of life just as the eagle does in a natural storm!

Also, notice the eagle doesn't fly out in the face of a storm with the attitude, *Well, I'm going to see if this works.* With that kind of attitude, he'd be destroyed.

Neither can *we* go out and face the storms and the circumstances of life that come our way with the attitude that we'll try the Word and see if it works. No! We must face every storm with confidence in the Word of God and with great boldness and fearlessness — just like the eagle!

Depend on God's Word
To Bring You Out!

The problem with some people is that rather than standing on God's Word and facing their troubles head-on, they're always looking for another way out.

For example, someone may get in a financial bind, and the first thing he does is run over to Grandma's house to see how much money she can give him. Then he starts trying to figure things out on his own, saying: "Well, let's see now. Uncle Johnny is always good for ten dollars. And Aunt Mary always had a soft spot in her heart for me. I believe if I butter her up, I could get at least fifty dollars out of her. . . ."

Sometimes that's the easiest way out. But I'll tell you something that someone once told me: If you go to the well too often, sooner or later it's going to dry up! *Then* what are you going to do?

No, you need to realize that *God* is the supplier of your needs (Phil. 4:19)! So you might as well learn how to use your faith wings now and start depending on God's Word to bring you through the storms of life!

Facing the Storm
In the Early Days of RHEMA

In the early days when we first started RHEMA Bible Training Center, there were many times that I had to use my faith for the things I needed. I never told anyone about it, but I had to believe God each day to meet my needs.

I'd get up and put on my best suit and tie, looking like I could buy the world, so to speak. And on the way to work I'd thank God in advance for a couple of dollars just to buy a hamburger, French fries, and a Coke for lunch! I didn't have anything in my pockets but my car keys and my driver's license. That was it, *period!* No "hide" money tucked away in my billfold for safekeeping — nothing!

In those early days of RHEMA, I had to face the storm and believe God to provide for my basic needs every day. But I thank God that I learned how to depend on God's Word in those early years. Otherwise, my wings wouldn't be as strong as they are today!

'I Believe God!'

Now when you're exercising your faith and believing God for something, the answer doesn't always come instantly. So the enemy will often come and try his best to get you to quit and to discourage you from standing on the Word.

In those situations you can do one of two things. You can become discouraged and downcast and lose your victory. Or you can stand your ground, face the storm, and say, "I believe God!"

That's what the Apostle Paul did in the Book of Acts on the boat headed for Rome. If you remember, a storm arose, threatening the safety of all the men onboard. But through an angel, Paul had received God's Word promising that no one's life would be lost even though the ship itself would be destroyed.

Now those men on the boat tried everything they knew to do, but the storm prevailed. It was so fierce that all hope of victory seemed to be lost.

Paul could have given in to despair and discouragement like the others. But instead he faced the storm and said, ". . . *I BELIEVE GOD, that it shall be even as it was told me*" (Acts 27:25).

And in the midst of *your* storm, you're going to have to do the same thing. You're going to have to stand boldly and say, "I believe God even as the Word has said!"

People may say, "That's too simplistic."

Well, it may be. But I'll tell you something, friend: It works!

As for me, I've made the decision that if God said it, *I believe it* — and that settles it!

---

[1] Col Stringer, *On Eagles Wings*, Col Stringer Ministries, Jacksonville, Fla., 1983, p. 8.

[2] Ibid., pp. 8-9.

Chapter 5
Be an Eagle Christian

We saw that there are two distinct characteristics about the eagle in the storm: 1) he shows utter *fearlessness* in the face of destruction, and 2) he has *the ability to soar*.

We need to become just like that — "eagle" Christians, fearless and confident in the face of adversity, snatching victory from defeat as we soar to greater heights!

You see, the eagle doesn't have an identity crisis; he's not searching for his identity. He knows what manner of creature he is and what he is able to do, whether it's hunting skillfully for prey or soaring majestically in the sky. And that's the way he lives.

But did you know that through the Word of God, you and I can know who we are too! We can know who we are in Christ and what we have in Him, where we're going in God, and how we're going to get there. And we can live in continual victory as we apply those spiritual truths to our lives. That's the way the *eagle Christian* lives!

But too many times I hear folks say, "I know what the Word says, but I just don't know whether I'm really an overcomer or not."

You see, it's not enough to just know the Word. You have to act like the Word is so; *that's* the only way to experience real victory. Otherwise, you'll continue to doubt and wonder, and your life will be filled with sadness, despair, want, and lack.

Now I am not saying that you're not a Christian unless you're living like an overcomer. Certainly you're a Christian if you've received Jesus Christ as your Savior, but I want to encourage you to be an *eagle* Christian!

Are You Living With the Sparrows?

Suppose you put a baby eaglet with a family of sparrows. Did you know that young eagle would probably grow up thinking he's a sparrow and acting like he's one? He may never know that he's an eagle. Yet within him all the time is the nature of a magnificent bird that has the potential to reach greater heights than a sparrow ever could.

Well, in the same way, *we* have all the potential of God's mighty power on the inside of us. Yet some of us are living with the sparrows instead of soaring with the eagles!

Friend, I want to challenge you to leave the lowlands of the sparrow mentality behind and ascend to the high places God has for you! I want to challenge you to get hold of God's Word and ride the winds of the Spirit to another level of faith that you've never achieved before.

It's entirely up to you. You can live your whole life at a lower plain with the sparrows, or you can soar up higher with the eagles!

Supernatural Strength

Other birds may fly with the eagle for a while, but the eagle is the only one that can soar to such great heights. No other bird can compare to the eagle in flight. Even in the midst of a storm, the eagle surpasses all others: While the turkeys scurry for cover on the ground, and the sparrows and other birds take refuge in their nests, you can look up and see the eagle still soaring in the sky!

We've been studying this magnificent bird that God created to learn some practical lessons we can apply to our lives. And one of the characteristics that the eagle is noted for is his amazing strength and ability in flight.

ISAIAH 40:29-31 (NIV)
29 He [the Lord] **gives STRENGTH to the weary and increases the power of the weak.**
30 Even youths grow tired and weary, and young men stumble and fall;
31 But those who hope in the Lord will renew their STRENGTH. They will soar on wings like eagles; they will run and NOT GROW WEARY, they will walk and NOT BE FAINT.

Notice the last part of Isaiah 40:31 says that as we soar on wings like eagles, we won't grow weary and we won't be faint. That's talking about supernatural strength.

If you think about it, it's normal for you to get tired or weary after doing something for a long period of time. Your natural strength and ability will eventually fail you because they're limited. They can sustain you for a while, but they can't give you any lasting momentum. But the power of God that dwells inside of you can!

You see, your ability to soar doesn't come from your own strength. It's not by *your* might or *your* power; it's by *His Spirit* (Zech 4:6)!

Your ability to soar above adversity comes from the strength of the Lord. And the Bible says that the joy of the Lord is your strength (Neh. 8:10). That's why you can face adversity with a smile on your face and a song of praise on your lips instead of a tear in your eye and a whine in your voice!

So begin to draw upon the power of God within you in every situation in life. Make a practice of speaking God's Word in faith, and trust in the supernatural strength of the Lord that is able to sustain you.

Soar to New Heights

Friend, because of the power in God's Word, we have the opportunity to excel in strength like the eagle. So let's not just be satisfied with where we are spiritually. Let's soar on to new heights as God has given us the ability in His Word.

I don't know about you, but I'm determined to be just like that eagle in the storm. That eagle was not moved by what he heard or saw because he knew he was able to soar above the storm. In the same way, I'm not moved by what I hear, see, or feel. I'm moved only by what I know!

What do I know? Well, for one thing, I know in Whom I have believed and am persuaded that He is able to keep me (2 Tim. 1:12)! And I know that even though I walk through the valley of the shadow of death, I will fear no evil. Why? Because God is with me (Psalm 23:4)!

The devil can bring anything he wants to try to bring against me. But by the authority of God's Word, I have the power and the ability to soar above any obstacle that he throws in my path.

So I'm going to hold fast to God's Word and soar with the eagles. I'm going to mount up with the wings of faith and experience God's best — because I know that's what God wants for me!

On the Wings of Faith

Life on the wings of faith is far from being dull. It's exciting; it's exhilarating! This is how the *eagle* Christian lives — soaring on wings of faith!

I want to encourage you to be an eagle Christian and soar on the wings of faith. When the storm clouds of life come bringing darkness and gloom to your world, have as much courage as the eagle and face them head-on!

Take the power of the Holy Spirit and the Word of God and soar above the darkness. Soar above the gloom. Soar clear above every cloud of adversity until you break through to the peaceful skies of victory where you can glide on outstretched wings in majesty and strength!

But it starts with your making a move. Move out of the nest of spiritual complacency and mediocrity and set your sights high in the Lord. Begin to develop your spiritual wings by spending time with the Lord in prayer and praise and exercising your faith in God's Word every chance you get. Then as you wait before the Lord, putting all of your trust in Him, you *will* renew your strength. You will soar on wings like eagles to reach your full potential in God!

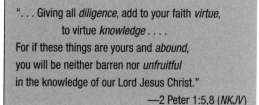